AN E̶r̶r̶ ENTR

"A Personal Development"

By

Dr John Mwansa Lukomona PhD

Dedication

I give a special dedication to my mother and father, who had initial input into my life helping me to be an independent thinker and hence later developed into an effective leader and entrepreneur. My sister, in Germany, said to me the other day, "parents trained us so well that we can go anywhere in the world and still make it in business and anything we touch. The business skills we developed in our early childhood were phenomenon, because of parental training and godly influence".

Disclaimer:

The view of the author on the mentioned individuals and organisations is not a reflection of their legal or natural disposition[1]. All scenarios are described as real life experience by the author and have no inclination to defame the character or overstate the character or promote their image but rather a mere narration of life experience. The book is also a text book for students on the entrepreneurship course; written to help candidates follow some lectures the author has been giving on the subject.

---

[1] A person's inherent qualities of mind and character.

ISBN: 9798611200544

Dr. John Mwansa Lukomona
"An Effective Entrepreneur", Edition 2.

Series: Education

Amaka Ya Bwingi Media Publishing Department and
West Midlands Open College, Press.

Edition 1: First released 9th May 2019, An Effective Entrepreneur

Edition 2: First released July 2020, includes an introductory
Chapter on Strategy.

Released in the United Kingdom

ENJOY AND LEARN

Contents

Preface

This book will help you become focused and motivated to develop your business idea from scratch to implementation; thereby helping you to have your first step in the real world of business.

The author has given attention to the emotional needs of readers and learners on entrepreneurship and business development. Other readers might actually think that this is a novel, worth reading, but in the process learn a lot more on how a business plan is written, the cost benefit analysis and general business characteristics an entrepreneur should develop.

This is the second book, Edition 2, on entrepreneurship since the launch of the John Lukomona Scholarship Scheme (JLSS), which funds in kind candidates who want to pursue the course within the West Midlands Open College.

The book is written to help many candidates who want a simplified narrative that can help them learn the basic steps to starting a business, including simple strategy.

Acknowledgements

First I acknowledge the support of my wife who humbly gave me space to dedicate time to writing this book.

I thank God for all my students; on the entrepreneurship, who have loved the style of my presentation and actually tease out the strength in me.

I further acknowledge all the people I have met in various networking meetings organised by Amaka Ya Bwingi[2] and the West Midlands Open College[3] and many other places where I had been for business development.

Above all let me acknowledge the presence of my Father, God for His Spirit that works; to energise me to do the work of teaching people through workshops and writing. Amen.

---

[2] www.amakayabwingi.org

[3] www.westmidlandsopencollege.co.uk.

CHAPTER 1

THE PROBLEM

One day I recollect, between 2006 and 2008, how many people walked up to me in Zambia, shortly after delivering what was an inspiring motivational talk on investment. At break time a few people volunteered to submit their business plans with a view to find funders for them? It was a humbling situation, which I did not expect to experience.

Who can just come and give you a business plan? This is a precious document. I didn't know many of the people in the auditorium, as this was a paid open conference, but you realise how much people would put their trust in a speaker or presenter. A stranger!

At that moment I realised that, while I perceived my conference as a mere platform to share information; participants saw it as a problem solving platform.

Each person as I gathered, later, came with a specific problem in mind which they believed that I could solve. Looking at the advert of my conference, in the media, it stated, "Interest free loans!!!" My concept of it was that people would come together and make financial groups and put money on the table to look for joint ventures. This was the message I was bringing in my motivational programmes in the UK amongst the Diaspora and across Africa, starting with Zambia.

I was amazed at the level of clarity of what these participants had in their own plans. The business ideas were so good that academically they would all tick the box.

My question was that; why couldn't some of these ideas kick off since they had been written?

Here is the catch! Are you ready? Why do you think people came to my meeting? The advert said,"Interest free loans!", and people responded in great numbers to this caption.

Here is the most important thing you have to know as a business person. People have problems in their lives in general, just like you; as you are reading this book.

Problems vary in degree, importance, and size. The one who endeavours to solve any one size of problem is the one who will get the proportionate reward.

For your business idea to succeed you need to identify what problem you are solving for anyone. It is this problem that people reward you for, with cash, in exchange. This is called sales. If a person sets up a business and no one seems interested, it is clear that, with a benefit of a doubt, the business idea is not solving any important problem at all.

Let us take for example the biggest problem we now have in the modern world. Communication has been one of the biggest problems ever and I recall sending a message, in those days, the fastest way was by telegram. This took at least 4 weeks. The coming of the Internet meant that the problem of speed and effective communication round the world has now been solved; that is why there are currently many subscribers and these people can never ever do without the Internet. The reward to the problem solver is a lot of money. Talk about Bill Gates, it will amaze you as to how much money his Microsoft business earned him, because it is associated with software and hardware; supporting a wide range of things including communication, which requires windows operating system; and more. What problem are you solving in your business or what do you intend to solve? I define an entrepreneur as a systematic problem solver who uses a legal business vehicle to deliver the required solution to the problem in hand, for people's benefit. In exchange the entrepreneur is rewarded with cash.

When you embark on the business world to run your own system, you must ask yourself the two big questions: 'What problem am I going to be solving, and secondly can I live on very little rewards while people get to know about my business?' Many an entrepreneur never seems to get started because of lack of faith to just do it. In business as soon as you identify a problem to solve, you must look at how that problem can be solved. Is it going to be solved through a commercial structure or charitable one? The way you structure the vehicle is important because it will mean that you can serve the customers better and thereby set the pricing structure as appropriate. In addition, and also very important; the government policies must be adhered to. Businesses don't just exist. Governments have to set up regulations round certain business types.

These are meant to regulate businesses so as to protect yourself and the consumers. A number of things have to be considered as you plan to go into business, or it may be that you are already in business and up to now you have not structured your business. You may still be using your personal bank account and there is no systematic record keeping, this book is for you to learn how to distinguish between yourself and the business. I tell you that you are missing out on a lot of incentives, well organised businesses have. In the Chapters that follow, we are going to discuss in detail how a business steps-out and become a house hold name and self selling. Although there isn't anything that sells itself, you can make it look like it is self selling. All you have to do is never stop making the selling effort. If you stop, eventually your competitor takes over some of your market share and over time your revenue drops. So be very careful with some phrases or sayings.

Today I would like you to write down, in clear terms, what exact problem are you solving in your business or if you have not yet started, what problem would you be solving?

You are an entrepreneur.

Chapter 2

I recollect, once a person said to me that his business was ready to go. The first question was, "What is the legal status of your business?"

"What is that?" Was the apt response! When you say this business is ready, it means either that you have already got a business plan in place as well as being decisive on what type of legal status it is.

Let us look at the various types of business status, which can be broken into:

A person who wants to operate as an individual, and taken all the liabilities of the business. This type of ownership is called a sole trader. A sole trade is someone who in a way makes all the decisions for the day to day running of the business and there isn't an official company registration and therefore you are not answerable to the general public.

Normally in most countries like the United Kingdom, you will be required to obtain the tax reference number for the purposes of tax. This number is called the UTR. In some other countries like Zambia it is called the TPIN. In each country there must be a government system that allows you to pay tax. Find out please.

Tax is paid at the end of a given trading period, where as a sole trader you complete self assessment (SA) forms to declare your income and associated expenses. I suggest that you find out from the local authorities in your own country how this is done.

Tax systems in your business are important to put in place, just at the time you are stepping out, although you won't need it until a year later, or 18 months in the future. In the UK they add 6 months on top to allow preparation of books before the final deadline of submission.

I can tell you that time goes very quickly; before you realise it, the tax man will issue you a penalty for having failed to declare your income once they find out. In England systems are automated and a letter of reminder comes way before the due date and then, finally, there is no letter until you see a penalty notice to pay £150.00 and still be required to submit, failure to which this value increases each year. The companies house, in the UK, in most cases will transfer your fee to a debt collector if you do not pay within their time limit. Have a very good accountant and it will save you money.

Become legal from the very start because it is not a good thing to have a bad record on you while you are trying to build a business.

I remember in my own experience how my legs went so cold that I had to call my accountant, when I received a tax determination from HMRC. I had not known about what I am teaching in this Chapter then. Thank God it concluded with a view that I had nothing to pay.

They wanted £45,000 in tax arrears! Wow!!! This is simply because I had no idea as to whether such a thing existed; paying business tax. Ignorance is not an excuse. If the finances, I later declared, had a merit for me to pay that amount of tax, I would be in debt to HMRC.

While you are reading this book, someone would have been reminded to pay their penalty, and I believe that you will never be in that position yourself.

I have met people who are very strong willed, and they believe that trading alone is the best. If you are that person then you can be a sole trader. However consider the level of risk.

Chapter 3

Thinkers and observers, like yourself; because you have an inclination to solving problems; your mind is wired such that on a daily basis you think of helping to fix something that isn't right round you or within the community you live in. This is called, in my definition, an entrepreneurial inclination to tease out a business opportunity. Probably business scholars when they read this book would find it very interesting and to the point.

You might have heard the adage that "opportunities exist everywhere". I agree. The reason this is so; is because we live in a world that is not so perfect; in religion; we say because man fell from grace-sin entered the world hence everything became corrupt and hence nothing functions perfectly. Someone has to fix it. You!

Many problems around you can be fixed through a design of products and services in your community. Any problem you notice is a potential business opportunity. These opportunities come at a time you do not expect them.

The question is how do you realise that a business opportunity is here? How do you spot it, and act on it?

The very reason that you are reading this book starts for you journey to fine tune your eyes and ears and feelings and discernment to perceive and detect a business opportunity.

I was in London speaking for an organisation over a period of time to a group of fantastic women; in business. The group was charged with expectation as I started talking about the course content. I realised after the ice breaker that many of them actually have had a business experience in the past and that some of them were just at the very beginning of their journey. A good number of them were in the third sector; charitable organisations.

Looking at the front row; there was a lady whose name I could not figure out; and therefore, never nominated her each time I addressed the group. I have a tendency to call people out by name, when I am teaching, which makes them feel important.

One day, I took the register so as to be guided and use it to call out names at random. Suddenly, before I could call the name out, this wonderful lady raised her hand and said to me quietly, "You have called out everyone by name, but you have never done so for me."

She just beat me to it. She continued, "I know most people don't know how to pronounce my name; this is how it is pronounced." She ended.

I learnt her name. When I closely looked at her business idea, it was clear she was into events management and organisation. "Oh I could actually organise an event for you and you come and speak. Sir, I note that you are a motivational speaker. Are you?" She had asked me. "Indeed" I replied. "I could tell from the way you are teaching, it is interesting." She appraised me.

Here is an opportunity so easily spotted by my student, just there in the class room. Her senses are tuned to detect an opportunity in that area where she is domicile for her type of business. Another way, many people see opportunities, is when there are many issues in a community, say; problems with delinquency. If this bothers you so much that you cannot sleep because you think that someone needs to do something about it, certainly an opportunity is looking at you. Start drawing up some ideas on how you think this can be solved. Once you are done with your idea, begin the process of consultation with like minds and appropriate authorities. Eventually you will structure this opportunity into an appropriate business vehicle to deliver it. Thereafter, you start to earn some cash for it.

In modern times there are many environmental issues; say recycling of wastes; plastics and many other things that go with it. This is a huge problem. Can you start to see any way in your area to address this problem which has posed a business opportunity? You must be open minded as not to restrict yourself to one area of your qualification; meaning if you are a nurse and you see an opportunity outside nursing; you close yourself off. No.

An entrepreneur is open and must know how to link with others when an opportunity poses itself. In the programme of the business development network; Amaka Ya Bwingi, there are four business pillars that we focus on: Promotion, Education, Linking, and Innovation. You must apply these; Promote this idea to some potential buyers (who need the solutions) and local authorities (regulators), link it with appropriate people who may have expertise to deliver; look at an innovative way to structure the opportunity and seek to educate yourself in it for the purposes of launching this business idea. Give it a time frame before you come to the actual launch. The opportunity although was outside your area of qualification, at the end of the period of developing it; you could have now found partners qualified in the area. Work together. You remain as the business owner with significant control but operationally the experts are running the show for you. You get paid your cash out of that opportunity.

How to detect opportunities is really embedded in the community problems.

What about retail? There are some areas in the United Kingdom and also your country; where many a people walk some good distance before they can find a retail shop. There is a good opportunity for anyone who wants to make money through retail; or sell the idea to someone whom you know who is in retail to set up. Get paid for the idea or find a role in the development of that retail shop to which you suggested. You can get paid a commission.

This way, can be a starting point for you to partner with people who are in the industry, and overtime to begin identifying opportunities where you can invest your money. There is Chapter 6, which deals with investing in other portfolios; there you will learn ways to invest.

In the meantime look at the reflection on the next Section. Reflection must be an ongoing attitude in you as an entrepreneur. Have a systematic way to take account of the past and review in detail. You will discover answers in the past experience. It will inform you of future possibilities.

Reflect

There are many instances that you may have had opportunities to go into a business that was ready to give you immediate returns, but because you thought, you were not qualified; you let the opportunity pass you by.

Take time to write down a review as to what held you back. Look carefully at the things you have written down. May be you could start by using the following: What was the situation; what was your role part in that situation; who was; a person if any that discouraged you and why; what was the reasons you couldn't take the opportunity? Did the environment where you live restrict you? Was it fear that restricted you? Was it lack of finance?

After the above review consider this: What can you now do, that you have extra knowledge and motivation? What strengths have you got now that would enable you to detect and take on certain opportunities or pass them on for a commission to someone? What is the driving force in you that would want to see you succeed? What is compelling you to achieve? How many opportunities do you now see given that you have learnt how they arise? Can you see many business ideas around you? Have you listened to the news recently?

Have you been to a business networking meeting recently? How many problems were shared by people you spoke to?

Listening to some property crash courses; there is something that I like; 'source and pass on the deal'. This is the phrase they use in the rent-2-rent business; where you find a property and package the deal and sell to another property investor; from a minimum of £2500.00 depending on the actual deal.

Fine tune your senses to detect a business opportunity, please. Act on one opportunity to start with, and then develop it successfully, just as I have focused on education till this day.

CHAPTER 4

COST BENEFIT ANALYSIS

When a business opportunity is spotted and acted on: The next step is to choose a business vehicle and finally launch that business to offer a service to the community. However, before you can start this journey; it is important to consider a number of areas; the costs and benefits.

The benefits normally are wholly focussed on financial, usually called fiscal. Naturally this must be a starting point otherwise you will run into serious financial difficulties, should you launch a business and invest all your earned resources, for a start up capital and at the end of the trading period you discovered that actually the business wasn't viable after all that. You had chosen a wrong model, legal structure and also operational style, because you did not take time to go through the cost benefit analysis. This is a very significant point and I want you be very meticulous about it.

If you have already started your business and you find that there are many issues that are affecting your business regarding profitability or other problems; please take it through these steps I am suggesting in this start up process.

The first benefit is the financial one, and the question we normally ask; 'Is the business idea viable?'

A very important formula that you must use is "**Revenue** take away **Expenditure**". If the answer is a positive, the likelihood is that this business is viable, at least on paper.

The key area in the above formula is **revenue**; the source of it, is **customers**.

Are there going to be enough customers to be able to give you that amount of money in exchange for your business services or products? To find out this type of information is now very simplified in the 21st century because of the Internet. You can use a wide range of survey software and send the link across to the target market. The results will be important to you.

The next step will be to look at the actual financial cost of running that business, and the standard key areas to consider are; the staff wages and salaries (because you need people to run the business for you). Some types of businesses require that an administrative officer is always in the office to be able to carry out general administrative work and also pick up phone calls. This administrative officer must not be you when you are planning or doing the cost benefit analysis. You must let each role be played by an expert in the field so that it frees you, to be you, in your own role, that way the business will be efficient.

Workout the figures of these wages and salaries and how many staff you would need in each role. Each industry is very different in the way the initial staff structure can be planned. Some of these roles would change, as the business starts to run and evolve, with changes in the sector.

The next section, of the expenditure in addition to the salaries and wages, is the **overheads** such as the cost of; premises, insurance, printing and stationery; travel, electricity, gas, water and other expenses. Find out in your industry the typical regular and ongoing intrinsic business expenses in your sector.

For example a typical table would look like this, as a financial schedule in Table 1:

Table 1: Financial Schedule

Details	Amount Annually
Salaries and Wages	
Director	£40,000.00
Admin officer	£20,000.00
Sub Total A	**£60,000.00**
Overheads	
Premises	£12,000.00
Insurance	£250.00
Printing	£3000.00
Transport	£1500.00
Utilities	£1200.00
Business Rates	£1100.00
Sub Total B	**£19,050.00**
Grant Total=A + B	**£79,050.00**

It therefore, means that you must have the capacity to make enough money to cover the cost of running that business in Table 1: Your business each year should bring in as a minimum £79,050, for you as the director and all your staff to get paid and still the business survives. If this is the case, you have a very good *cash machine*.

To sustain this cash machine you need your customers to give you minimum revenue of £79,050 from selling. This is the income of your business.

If you can work with these figures, while controlling your expenditure very well, by shopping around for say; insurance, utilities, printing and stationery, even changing the sizes of vehicles you use in your business you can have a small gross profit before tax.

In the subsequent years you can make a good profit as you become more and more experienced in running the business; by reaching out to more customers and many of them would come through word of mouth; because of the **quality** of your services and products. We will discuss more on this in the section that deals with customer service.

Mathematically;

Profit/Loss = Revenue – Expenditure

If the Revenue is greater than Expenditure, you have a **profit** and if the Expenditure is greater than the Revenue you have a **loss**. Normally at the stage before tax we call it **gross** profit. After tax it is called **net** profit. If there is a loss there is no tax to pay, because tax is paid as a certain percentage of the gross profit, after the allowable expenses have been adjusted by Inland Revenue. Your accountant should deal with these areas; so no cause for worry.

Breakeven point is where you make no loss or profit but have recovered all the money you put in the business, and there is still enough remained to cover all your costs to continue running the business. If your profit margin is 20% of the costs of running say of £79,050 your actual profit will be £1,581; which can be growing year after year. If you are a start up, this could be the actual capital you require to start the business; plus the cost of equipment if needed. So you will add that cost and define it as the capital required.

The key point to note is; can you pay yourself, £60,000 per year and all your staff? Can your business meet all the legitimate expenses?

If the answer is yes, then the business idea is a bankable one, or simply viable. The security is in the uptake. The uptake means those who are ready to buy from you. If you can have that guarantee then you are winning. Go for it.

If the answer to the above analysis leaves you with not enough buyers to cover the legitimate costs you must not do it.

There are some business solutions which are of government interest because they are partly solving the community's pending problem which government wants to see solved. In this case it could be that; with the commercial model you have the government can actually come in through PPP or as the case might be where certain costs are borne by them or they inject a good some of money in kind say; provides land; buildings etc. Now this will take off from your business shoulders a whole weight of the cost for you to be able to make that profit for sustainability.

We covered in a nut shell the fiscal benefit analysis to a basic degree. I would like to look at the non fiscal benefits and costs.

A few years ago, I had a chance to reconnect with an old friend of mine. The gentleman had not stayed with his family for over five years, the reason being, him and his wife decided to pursue their careers. One of them got a job in another country and the other in a totally different country and continent.

Amazing arrangement! Can you survive this type of cost? You do not see your family regularly and you have to save up once every year to travel and see your family for five years. Once in a year to do things; you kind of start the courtship all over each year to fit in the family. This situation is a non fiscal cost.

Some businesses would require you to stay away from your family for many months. Can you handle that? If the answer is yes, go for it. If no, find an alternative way.

Other factors could be that of family movement; would the business bring out a positive outlook on your family where they can start to access better medical facilities, education and so forth? Would it improve your status quo or worsen it? If it is positive, go for it. Otherwise find an alternative.

Questioning yourself and developing a good attitude towards your life's activities will help you shape your destiny and end well in the set business objectives.

Environmental costs and national security are a big factor in modern day business launches. In recent times in the UK Haewui has dominated the news because of security issues. These are costs that the proposed business services have had to be exposed to. In your own business idea, look at the effect on the environment and the need for planning permission. Just by looking at the present environmental issues you can determine as to whether your government will allow permission in the first place.

Regulators are so important in certain types of businesses and therefore, it is advisable to start researching that aspect.

I recall many years ago when our own business group started to entertain the idea of importing food stuffs from Zambia into the UK to serve the growing Zambian and African community. The first port of call before we started to import was DEFRA. DEFRA deals with all types of food imports that are allowed and not allowed into the United Kingdom. This is an interesting aspect because if you do not check this requirement you could spend money to order and when the food arrives; it would be rejected entry, and may be destroyed or shipped back or dealt with according to the regulations.

What are legal requirements in your industry of interest? Find out the information and it might be that you will need a special license.

CHAPTER 5

BUSINESS PLANNING

I rung my brother, who lives in Germany, the other day and the first thing he said was that, he remembers many years ago when I spoke to his team and our family; I emphasised planning for the future and looking at it visionally.

He was happy that many years on, he is still following his plan regardless of where he is domicile. He also referred to our family members and how they have settled very well, because they were present in these business talks on planning and following your God given idea and plan.

A business idea that touches you so much because you want to meet a community need, is God given; that is what we believe. Then you can have as many off shots as is possible.

The way you develop this idea starts with your pen and paper. Start planning! When? Today!

You have the time; create it by giving up something, say, television, like my wife who watches too much of it.

Train yourself, to adapt to a new discipline, as a business person. People think to become a business owner you have plenty of free time to do everything round you. NO!

It is time to become more committed to this new baby called the business. You have to have that commitment. Things don't just do themselves. You have got to do something about it. "I woke up round 49 3.00am and started writing this Chapter 3 to 5 of this book! What were you doing?"

"I realised that this book needs to be completed because my students need it and therefore no one will complete it for me. I walked down stairs from the third floor where the comfort of my bed is and left my wife there to write. This is what it takes to be a business person who can succeed. In a few hours when I finish writing, at 10:30am, I will go to church."

What do you put in a business plan and why?

In teaching we say a lesson plan must be written such that if you were away and someone else comes to cover your lesson, they must be able to follow your plan and deliver it, just as you planned it. So is a business plan, it must be implementable.

When you draw it and you employ people they must work according to plan. The business plan will be translated into job descriptions, because people must work accordingly to achieve the goals of the business as planned. Of course some stuff will change when you start operations because of many factors. There will be adjustments but not completely so as to replan. In fact you will only know if the adjustment needs to be made, if there was a plan in the first place. A reference point is your business plan.

A business plan is a document who's first and most important audience and implementer is you the business owner. You are not writing that business plan for an investor. Ask yourself this big question.

If you the owner cannot invest that business plan, who do you think will risk the money and invest in your idea? Putting money in the drain? Would you do that? So if your thinking was like that, please, "delete" it now and start thinking afresh.

There is no one out there, with money, looking to throw it at some wishful thinker. Agreed? Good.

The first and simple outline of your business plan would look like this:

<u>Content List</u>

1. Introduction

Executive Summary

2. Context or background
3. Business Status
4. Vision
5. Market Analysis
6. Developmental Objectives
7. SWOT
8. Investing in other portfolios
9. Financial Projections
10.   Appendix

The above content list is not exhaustive you can add more depending on the nature and structure of the intended business. Let's work with the above list and explore more thoughts.

The Introduction, introduces the reader to what is contained in the whole business plan and normally will be in the form of an executive summary; which is an abridged business plan. The reason for this; is to give at a glance what your business plan looks like. It will enable the reader to have a very quick overview before they start looking at it in detail. Some business plans can have many hundreds of pages; in phases.

The context or background, is the back drop of the business? What has been happening in the area where you are launching or intend to launch your business? What are the factors that are prevalent and also influenced your need to set up this business in that location? It could be general economic outlook, or things that have happened and may have caused the collapse of system in your country, which as a result, have created an opportunity for you to start this venture in order to provide a new service or product.

The business status is the type of legal vehicle you have chosen. Is it a sole trader, private limited company; by shares or private limited company by guarantee, public limited company, partnership, community interest company with shares; charitable organisation etc? Check the types of legal structures allowed in your country of domicile.

The reason for a legal structure becomes apparent, for classification in terms of tax and how profits are used. In a private limited company by shares and also public limited company, profits are shared between the shareholders. If a company makes a profit legally these monies can be put into the pockets of share holders without any issues at all. If your company is private limited company by guarantee or a community interest company (CIC) or charitable organisation, any profit the organisation makes must be put back into the organisation and not in the pockets of the directors. The directors and others only get a wage or contract invoices paid for their services they render to the company under this legal status. Under this structure there is no share, it is illegal, of the profits; which are normally called the **surplus**.

For any organisation with 'limited' by legal status, it means all business matters are separate from the individuals running it, including the bank account which must be opened in the name of the company and not the individuals who started it. The liabilities are also limited to the business and no personal effect would be taken into consideration in case the business winds up or has losses. When choosing a legal status for your business, this is a good point to consider by looking at any potential thing that can go wrong, if it can be handled by you as an individual or through a separate entity like a limited company.

A sole trader is one, where you as an individual decide, to take on all the liabilities of the business and is the only person with significant control for the whole decision making process. Liability is not limited to your business and therefore if there is a debt, your personal effects can be claimed upon, and sold to recover the debt by whosoever you owed anything. Councils are very good at chasing sole traders, and their bailiffs follow you to your house. Therefore, you might want to consider a limited company structure.

A sole trader also has no formal registration with companies' house, for example in the United Kingdom. Please check the date of this book; things could have changed, as regulators are always making reviews. At least as at current time, the only legal registration a sole trader requires is that you register with HMRC (for those in the UK) or any taxation board you have in your country you are domicile. In the UK you will be allocated a Unique Tax Reference number for tax purposes.

Take note that all company types regardless of legal status have a UTR[4]. They all need to pay business tax when they make a profit or surplus. If there are

---

[4] Unique Tax Reference

any exemptions the tax authority will notify you about it.

Vision, inclusion in the plan, is very essential because it is in fact the driving factor for the destination of the business. What are the key components that help to formulate a vision for your business?

Some examples of vision statements include; "*To be an eco-friendly business; value addition business; community sensitive business; the best producer of;.....; a profitable business that will open up shareholding to employees and so forth*". The vision section can also be in bullet points if you have more than one aspect, of what you want to be like, in your business vision.

How you run your business to deliver products and services should be such that, they are leading to the vision on a daily basis; to became or meet the vision statements that you have stated. In the delivery scheme are you implementing systems that will make sure that you are eco-friendly?

For example one of our vision statements is to be a platform where young people gain work experience. At the West Midlands Open College and all forms of business regardless of name evolution, we have maintained and proactively created space, at least for one work experience for a young undergraduate; especially in finance and business administration. This way we meet one of our vision objectives. We contribute to the development of the younger generation who are looking to complete their degrees through meeting the required work placement.

Board meetings must conclude deals, by considering all possible business plan objects, including the vision statement.

These things are not just a literature record. In business they must be followed. If you can demonstrate this type of performance and in the future you needed an investor, to come in; they will look at your historical performance and how well you have implemented your own business plan. This will be a good indicator on how secure and profitable their money might become if invested in your business. Also it must be mentioned that people invest in people. When a person seeks to invest in your business, first and foremost they are looking at you as a person. If they like you and they think you are the right person and the drive you have, if supported can make the business grow, the investor will give you money in exchange for equity. All about vision!

One of the things I invest in when I start a new group of students on the entrepreneurship course, especially those who have joined the waiver scheme; John Lukomona Scholarship (JLS) Scheme, is to find out their vision and business idea. I ask them to articulate this in 60seconds. If you are clear about where you want to go, it is very easy to follow you; after you say it within a minute. Lifts in a building do not take more than five minutes and people normally don't talk to each other in a lift because they are all strangers. They happen to meet there because they need the lift to their floor. What if you just strike a conversation for any reason, and you suddenly realise; this is Warren Buffet; what will you say your vision and idea is in 45seconds- his floor is approaching and he has to quickly dash out? Think about this situation.

I will not discuss every content list in this Chapter as I would like you to research more and refine your own business plan, but let me discuss briefly the **products** and **services**.

The core area and the actual driver of your business and the reason it is called the business is because of what you are offering: Is it a tangible **product** or a **service**?

You must be very clear and to the point. If a person asks you, "What does your business provide?" Your answer should be prompt, for example; "we sell handmade leather handbags for women; of all age groups"; "we sell copper ore to *mining* processing companies"; we provide private lessons to students doing mathematics at GCSEs"; I sell knowledge in form of motivational talk workshops every Thursday at the Enfield library, mainly to adults who have issues with low self esteem", in that manner. Clear and to the point!

At this stage we are not interested in the process of how you do it, unless your service cannot be mentioned without including a process statement for clarity purposes. Like one of the examples of selling knowledge because many people won't understand that you can actually sell knowledge. For this reason you explain with a statement of process; through motivational talks. Motivational talk is a very familiar thing and most people would say, "Oh, ok, I know. How do you sign up to attend?" Bingo! You have got a potential customer.

Therefore, when you are drawing your business plan, this section must be the clearest section of the business plan. Write it as simply as you can and end there. It is good practice to ask a friend or a business colleague to see if the way you have written the business products and services would make them understand what the business is selling? Or is it vague.

Now have a look at your services/product section of your plan and check if it aligns with what we are discussing in this book. Take time to discuss it with a class mate or even your friends. Normally asking your husband or wife is not the best idea, because spouses at times do not seem to agree professionally. Please ask someone else who will give you a balanced view. Your spouse is good for something else and not business discussions of this nature; except where you share a common goal in business, please by all means discuss.

Chapter 6

One of the biggest questions that you have asked yourself when running a business is:

"This business I have set up and the money I am earning from it, what would become of it afterwards?"

The question is too broad and vague for a reason; what would become of it? It does not make sense. Indeed the answer is surely that. It does not make sense if you set up a business and are earning a good salary out of it, but when you are tired and lost interest to run it what next?

To help your security; you must learn how to invest some extra cash elsewhere; so that you can be earning passive income while you have the capability to make cash come into your hands from your business. This is the first step.

One of the ways to do this securely is to look at buying stocks or bonds in existing regulated platforms, through stock brokers. You can search and find out which stocks have a potential to grow significantly well over 5 to 10 years. These are monies that can be paying back to you once earned; reaping in multiples.

I remember in 2006, I gave a workshop on the concept; invest once and reap multiple (IORM). I am sure many who attended that conference in Kabwe[5] , have since climbed the ladder of investment and are doing very well. Find a very good company that is listed on a stock market. It could be the London Stock Exchange or Lusaka Stock Exchange or as the case

[5] In Zambia, central province.

might be. Off shore stocks outside the western world can be very profitable. Try and explore this route and decide that each month you will buy stocks from as little as 100 till you reach 10,000 of them, over a certain period of time. If you are risk averse you can put a huge lump of sum in one go and wait on its maturity. One of the fine years we made 420% capital gains profit on some stocks on the LuSE, through a group investment. It was marvellous.

This way you have diversified your earned cash to grow it somewhere else other than your business. The risk is out in another pot rather than your own business. Business is a risk and those who take risks are the ones that make it. If you are afraid; you will never cross the bridge.

There are other areas such as government bonds; futures; unit trusts and more. Take a short trip to your bank and ask the investment bank manager to give you an appointment and learn more of what they offer.

You might want to start with the simplest ISAs and grow from there as you become more experienced in investing.

Now look back at when you started writing your business plan; you had a thought of finding an investor-someone who has money; they want to grow by putting it in your business. This is the same position you have now reached that you have some cash saved somewhere. Instead of that cash sitting in an ordinary bank account earning 0.5% PA, you could risk that money by investing in another business run by someone else, and then you ask for equity.

What is equity? This is the share of the business, for example if that business you put money in agrees to give you 15% equity it means that, each time their business makes a net profit £10, 000, you will get 15% of £10,000 to come into your pocket as a share holder. So invest once and reap multiples.

In the agreement, the owner might want your advice as well to be included, if you have any expertise in the area; or they just simply needed your capital input of finances.

This way you find that you are doing well while running your own business. Money is coming to you passively.

Currently I am looking to invest in a totally new business outside my area of interest because it came on my desk as an opportunity. Someone came to my workshop on property and they ended up discussing with one of my mentors the possibility of selling their own business. Now it has really matured and I was invited to be a director on the new business when the sale is completed, so that I can render skilful advice and confidence boost, with a nominal financial contribution. The business is highly liquid and contracts are present too. It is a good thing.

The vehicles you can invest in are those which are profit making businesses; legally registered as limited companies by shares. The companies you access through stock markets are public limited companies (plcs) these are legally allowed to ask for capital input from the public; while private limited companies by shares can only obtain capital input from individuals you know, including family and friends. You cannot advertise in the public domain for shares for a private limited company by shares.

Therefore, as an entrepreneur you have to have knowledge on how else you can grow your money as you make it in your own business.

Other portfolios could be in property where you participate in buying to let, where you surrender the property to a letting agency that helps to do all the management of it, including collecting rent. The letting agencies, depending on what level of services, can charge up 12% of your rentals from the property.

Chapter 7

The magic of self motivation, when you start your own business, consists in knowing when to pay yourself handsomely and when to pay yourself at a minimum wage.

This journey starts with scaling down on your former life style before you became a business owner, scaling up on certain financial habits in some areas.

For example as an employee for another company that you worked for, you knew exactly how much you would get at the end of each month and you could easily borrow on your credit card and later reimburse over time. In short you lived excessively above your means because someone sold you extra cash which you were allowed to spread over many months;

even years, if you have entered in what is called as perpetual debt.

When you become a business owner, the honeymoon ends; because you are the boss and have to look after everyone in the organisation.

Keeping your employees happier is a very big success ingredient you can ever achieve. Pay them in good time so that the business does not suffer. For your supplier of services who are not employees, usually the legal system allows a 30 day credit period. Try and work within that time frame. It applies to self employed staff who invoices you for their services rendered, also.

Every milestone must be celebrated and if you get used to this habit; you will find that doing business is a great joy. What do you celebrate?

The very fact that you have started is worth thanking God for; therefore, call a small gathering of friends or family to celebrate the start of the business. Remember the journey to this point. A change of life; a new era!

The next thing that you celebrate is the first customer that paid you. This is an amazing feeling when you first opened those doors to your business and lo there walks in a happy customer paying you for the service. This is a sweet thing. Cash!

Celebrate the end of the first month regardless of how much you have paid yourself and those that are working for you, this will bring a sense of progress and achievement in a step wise manner. Do not wait for the "big-bang-sell" of amounts at the close of the first month, but be happy with the initial revenue. You must know that while customers are walking through your doors; other business are filing bankruptcy, while others are struggling just to get one customer to enquire for anything at all.

I remember when I re-opened the tuition department for young people in the college after many years of silence. It appeared as though no one would be interested. Then suddenly there it was. One of my tutors was so shocked that within days of her saying to me, "Dr John, I depend on you to keep me busy", she said this with an air of profound fear mixed with a bit of diminished hope; but wanting this programme to work. " Well, let's all depend on God, as we do our bit to market", I replied trying to shift the weight of responsibility to my Father God, because I didn't want this tutor to come and say where are my teaching hours?

A week later and running into the second, she called me that she has not got time anymore. Her hands were too full! She needed some time with her family. Wow!!

This was a very big breakthrough in the market where we entered to compete with existing players. Our business model attracted so many customers such that we had to advertise for more teaching jobs. This is a milestone to celebrate because customers make a business and in fact they put a signature of authenticity.

The other things that you should celebrate a-lot are the word of mouth referrals, when they come. This is the most important time of your business because people have liked what you offer for them to refer others. Think about this. It is important to realise that someone who came to buy off you, would be able to recommend another person, because they were very happy with your products or services. Mathematically; it means that the other people who are linked to the referred; will also likely to become added customers.

Celebrate the good name that is developing. The way you do it is up to you. You are slowly becoming a household name a thing that is not so easy to achieve. In celebrating the good name invite those people, who referred a person to you, for free food and say thank you. Allow them to come with a friend; as a added thank you and you will discover that, this celebration just adds more customers to you.

Celebrate the first accreditation or membership of a professional body, or any partnership that has developed as a result. Many of these partnerships are a true signature that your business has come as a good thing and other organisations want to work with you.

There are so many things that you can shortlist worth having a party on an excuse to invite people to it. When people turn up to attend, always have a small interlude where you verbally speak out your thanks and joys of achieving it today; and present to people what you exactly do as a business and show them how they can get involved with yourselves. Always use the words 'let us work together to make our community a happy community. We as a company we seek to contribute through our services and products to help community become stronger and better together'. This type of talk is inclusive and makes people feel a part of it.

Think and reflect where you are now. Have you become a better person with respect to entrepreneurship? Have you made any progress towards the journey in actualising the vision of your business? Whatever stage you are at now, please plan a party to celebrate and thank God. Invite friends and families. They will first think that you are out of mind, but what you are actually doing is that you are declaring openly; that you are on the journey to your successful destination and how you look today is not what is ahead of you. Better things are ahead of you. They are looking at an employer and a very good problem solver whose class is amongst the champions of the business world.

Chapter 8

THE MINDSET OF AN ENTREPRENEUR

Cognitive, is thinking and reasoning. How do you think? Many actions, apart from a reflex, start with a thought pattern. The third dimension of a person is noticed in the way they react and pass decisions then you know who the person really is.

Adverse situations are a very good time to know the true person behind the ones that you normally see, on a daily basis.

"Oh! No! I didn't know that John was like that!" You would exclaim. "John just surprised me because he stormed out of the meeting that put him on the spot for cross examination during the board meeting on a certain decision he made a few months ago!" All these years you have never seen John act like that.

The adverse situation has really got deep into John's true third person; the actual processor has come out.

When you see greater difficulties in a nation and your immediate community, what goes through your mind? Do you join the large majority of mourners and protestors? Or do you incline towards a solution orientated mind set? Or do you simply brush off and think the situation will just disappear someday? Or do you plan to pack up and go somewhere and settle in some greener pastures?

Or you think; it is the politicians again, and you switch off the television set; the next polling day is coming so that you can remove some people out of office? Or do you take it on your spouse and start shouting verbalising the problems that are prevalent?

Or do you sit down and map out an investment programme that can potentially start to address some of the economic down run?

By now you might have found your position. Let me intimate to you; that great thinkers rise to the challenge, when things in a particular economic area are not as perfect as they should be. Enterprises are born during these hard times, and they tend to succeed, because they present an exit.

The market is so ready that anyone who provides a solution closer to the actual ideal is guaranteed, to have many customers and have steady income in their pockets.

Here is a dire situation that happened in the country I come from, Zambia. During the 80s, Zambia went through very big economic difficulties; rising shortages of essential commodities and services.

Many a people as a result hated the government whom they called the PIG. The PIG is an acronym for the Party and Its Government, as the incumbent president used to call it, when reading out publicly certain changes.

While many people were complaining and protesting; some of my age mates and friends took to retail and wholesaling. What? Where would they find what to sell because the whole country had come to a standstill! I witnessed it, because that time I had just gone to University.

These friends of mine; discovered a secret. They caught trains and travelled across the borders into Botswana and Zimbabwe. One of them I remember got a flight to the United Kingdom.

What did they go there to do? They went to see how people lived. They found out that everything Zambia didn't have; these nations had. So they worked out legally how to buy in bulk all these items and bring them to the country.

They found it too demanding to buy and retail; so what they did was to work differently. They first went around the country, within Zambia, to the known shop owners and collected a guarantee for the uptake[6] . They did it in form of an advanced deposit of finance. Each of the shop owners will give them prepaid purchase orders.

Easy! They went to purchase in huge quantities at wholesale price (most times they bought from retailers on the high street, ironically) and off loaded to these

---

[6] Customers or someone who can buy off you.

shop owners, in Zambia, at a mark up[7] , and because there was an acute shortage of these commodities in the country, people queued to buy at any meaningful retail price.

The wholesalers; my friends, and the retailers; shop owners began making staggering profits.

They created a solution in an economy where there was acute shortage of essential commodities.

They made money. I witnessed it. While still at university, I would visit one of my friends, he was able to afford luxuries at the age of 21, which many an African youth could never have!

You must be solution orientated as an entrepreneur. This is the only way you can

---

[7] Money you add on top to make a profit.

make that progress in the business world, which is posed with many a problem.

During a recession just as in the example above; entrepreneurs can grow exponentially. The excess profit that you may make; can now help set up systems where you create charitable organisations to help those with special needs. I have seen people who can't make a dime out of any business idea; but they want to set up a charity in the hope that someone will give them money to help others. I do not understand this logic myself.

Set up a charity within the reach of what you can do, first to help others, by yourself; then invite financiers to add capacity to reach more people; after you evidence what you have achieved by your initial charitable efforts from your own resources.

One of the reasons why many charities or NGOs[8] don't achieve is because the initiator is looking for money to support once own livelihood.

---

[8] NGOs, stand for Non Governmental Organisations, which are charities.

Chapter 9

FLY

An effective entrepreneur, flies the best route ever to success, and doesn't fly first or business class, because an entrepreneur loves the hundreds of customers in the economy class where money is.

Numbers in people, make a business tick. If you are introvert and you cannot engage with people, find a very good marketing person or an outreach face that is good with people.

One thing that I do very frequently, is take walks to meet people on the street; visit partner businesses and share some support and just lend a hear to know what success stories and struggles they have. Become a visible person and eventually people feel safe with you and would like to buy from your business as a preference from their next door neighbour, who provides the same exact service, may be even better quality than you.

Customers would prefer you because you are visible and can easily be spoken to at anytime. I have used the method of visibility and it's made people come to the college for anything at all.

One lady came with a certificate and showed me that she saw another person with the same certificate. That person said to her that she was in very safe hands because Dr John is a good man.

I didn't even train the lady but another tutor did it. They have seen the chief executive in the street and talking to people very nicely and just involved in their affairs in a positive way. When people see the college logo they think about me in a good way.

Richard Branson is a very visible fellow and you always see him in adventures with people and the guy looks at home with everybody! That personification of a brand is a good thing to learn in business.

Can you develop the personification of your own business by moving from the 'business class to the economy'?

Chapter 10

STRATEGY

To fly in entrepreneurship when running a business, you require more entrepreneurial skills than you have just learnt in this book. The scope of this book is limited, therefore, I recommend that you obtain much more advanced books or follow my next series on the subject matter that addresses high level business techniques and ways of doing things.

Ideas are drawn from many successful entrepreneurs; business men and women including some of the things I have tried in my own businesses, too, such as the West Midlands Open College.

In this Chapter, I will just touch on the surface to introduce the thought on strategy.

Have you wondered why many businesses suddenly close after a period of growth and dominance in the market? There are some brands, which you used to hear about but all of a sudden after a few years they disappeared as if they never existed. Do you recall the Blackberry, Nokia and many other brands of phones, you no longer hear about, even though they are still in operation?

You will discover very soon that your own business will have a counterpart trading in exactly the same products or services as you are doing. While you think there is no problem with it, eventually you find that; many of your known customers will stop visiting you, in preference to the new comer.

You really do not want to move away from the area and start afresh somewhere else, do you? This might cost you a lot more than if you stayed and did something **differently** in your business; to attract more customers and even win the old ones back to yourself.

I have noted that in the West Midlands Open College, we tend to keep customers for a long time and these very customers keep referring more and more people to us. What do we do very well or differently?

We hear from people saying; a friend of mine said you should go to Dr John; he is a very nice person.

Dr John is not the only member of the college, but he is the voice of the college; a person whom any customer speaks to when applying to enrol. Dr John spends a lot of time talking and laughing with applicants and jokes a lot.

One of his jokes and appraisal goes like, "Wow, you sound like a rich person!"

And many people shout at the end of the line saying, "I receive it!"

The thing is that the college knows the target market and their aspirations. Another phrase normally used when parents ring to enrol their children on the tutorial programme is;

"Here we make your children into professors; so be aware that we will call your child a professor!"

Again you will hear at the end of the line, a response, 'Yes, that's what I want. These children here are doing nothing, just playing games on the computer'.

Then the conversation would continue like this; "Do not worry, as you are talking to the college; the problem is already solved! Can we speak to the professor you want to enrol, please?"

At that point it is so difficult for the applicant to turn down whatever you will offer, including the price. Once a conversation is struck with the candidate a raptor is formed at inquiry. They don't want to go anywhere else.

When quoting the price for tuition the college quotes first the value addition group fee, saying if you have say 3 children they can all come on the 2hr session and just pay a £50.00. This in the applicant's mind sounds too good to be true, because the calculations goes like £50.00 divided by 3 equals £17 approximately per child and this is just about £8.00 per hour. Wow!!

Oh no I have only one child who is in serious need of support while others are okay. "Yes we understand that, but do you have to wait for others to be in serious need for them to join or you want them to maintain and increase their professorship?"

The natural answer will be okay, its better they keep up the good work; with potential to enhance, with extra support.

Then we encourage them, if there are any financial issues, to have these sessions regularly on weekly basis; to try once every two weeks instead, with a promise to a lot of homework and access to our e-learning, 24/7.

Our e-learning[9] has all the sessions the college teaches and access to more other educational links.

This strategy makes the customers stay with the college. Although they try to go elsewhere, they find flat over there, the conversations are too professional, no emotions and no concerns for the whole family and no special offers. Their principal

---

[9] Can be created on www.westmidlandsopencollege.co.uk

is far-fetched and never interacts with customers and at the front desks; they don't know the person who even owns the business; and therefore they can't negotiate. The college's strategy is negotiations and concernment for the family.

When you join the West Midlands Open College it is like you have come to a family of real people, whom you can relate to; and people being social creatures tend to like this type of set up.

Furthermore, as customers stay longer many of them discover that there is an offer to do work placement with career progression, which is because the West Midlands Open College is very friendly and flexible and has a quick route to making decisions, and can create job opportunities very quickly.

The website is simple and has many images of **real** people having fun at graduation and more; so that whoever was referred by a friend, when they visit it; the same message relayed over the phone is repeated on the site through the images of people they know whose images are on the website.

Someone said that, "I saw from the college website, there are many happy people on it, including the mayor attending the ceremony." The archives over years of graduation depict the same feel.

This strategy is unique to the college, within the area of target, in keeping customers. You can almost say West Midlands Open College has a **blue ocean** strategy.

I live this question with you as an entrepreneur: What is strategy?

I would like you to define what strategy means to **you** and **your** business. In the above example a strategy would involve in how you fit your services or products with the market making adjustments to avert competition or making competition irrelevant, whereby you can even stay within few metres of your competitors and still draw more customers, who become loyal to you, to the extent that they feel and want to defend you and your business. You become a household name.

Just in closing on the West Midlands Open College; a gentleman who lived in Russia visited his home country Ghana; and there he told his family that he wants to move to the United Kingdom for a change.

"You must go and live in Birmingham near the West Midlands Open College; and here is their number. Call and ask for Dr John. He will guide you on career options and what to do in the UK." They insisted.

We liked the story we did not just train this gentleman in his course of interest, but also gave him a, part time paid, job because we discovered that he was very skilled in information and communication technology and could also handle customers.

On one hand, we fulfilled one of our core values and on the other hand, we put a smile on the face of this new immigrant to the UK.

What is your strategy?

The next book on strategy especially those candidates doing our degree in entrepreneurship at the Lukomonah John

University[10], will benefit by it, even those doing the full diploma of the entrepreneurship course, at West Midlands Open College.

By and large apply any of the knowledge in the book to your business. Dig deep and think about; what and how you can do it. Customers are essential and therefore, you need a very good strategy to serve and keep them.

---

[10] Visit www.lju.co.uk

Other books by the Author:

Every Zambian Is a Millionaire Part I

Every Zambian Is a Millionaire Part II

Zambia in Prophecy

Effective Teaching

A Note of Hope for Young People

Symptoms of a sick business

Every African Is a Millionaire

All are available on www.amazon.co.uk

Printed in Poland
by Amazon Fulfillment
Poland Sp. z o.o., Wrocław

63321910R00061